In Love Again & Always

Love Poems by
Carol Lynn Pearson

In Love Again
& Always

Love Poems by
Carol Lynn Pearson

CFI
Springville, Utah

ISBN 13: 978-1-59955-042-8

Published by CFI, an imprint of Cedar Fort, Inc.
2373 W. 700 S., Springville, UT, 84663
Distributed by Cedar Fort, Inc., www.cedarfort.com

Cover design by Nicole Williams
Cover design © 2007 by Lyle Mortimer
Edited and typeset by Erin L. Cameron

Printed in the United States of America

10 9 8 7 6 5 4 3 2 1

Printed on acid-free paper

Most of the poems in this collection
were published in *I Can't Stop Smiling*, 1984,
Parliament Publishers, Salt Lake City, Utah.

♥ Contents

I Can't Stop Smiling

And if I can't stop
Smiling,
Will the sweet paralysis spread?

Will it move down the muscles
Of my heart and lungs
Until all systems
Freeze or burst?

Has anyone ever
Died of delight—
Or do I get to be
The first?

Resurrection

Was it a healing
Or a resurrection?
I couldn't see.

I only know
Some lovely part of me
Had closed its eyes
And covered its face
With the final sheet.

And then,
Shocked into breath
By that brief, amazing touch—
It moves again.

The Wave

I go about my business
And I remember that you love me.

I pick up a spoon
And the knowledge washes over me
Like a warm wave.
By the time I put the spoon down
Another wave has hit.

Like the chills when I had the flu
(Only so much nicer)
It goes like that all day long.

That warm wave—
On, and on, and on.

The Eclipse

You moved
Moonlike and precise
Between me
And my pain.

Orbits froze.
A universe fell.

Only space
And the soft
Round circle
Of your love
Remain.

The Secret

You are a secret
I tell myself
When I'm alone.

I listen
Wide-eyed
And open-mouthed
To news that never
Gets old.

You are a secret
That I burst
With knowing.

Our Island

Could we create an island,
You and I?

We are so firmly fixed now
On so firm a continent
Where the population is high
And pressing.

But could we come up somehow
With a man-made moat
And a very private boat
And beach enough for two?

I could deal with my days,
I think,
Manage the fours
And the twenties
And the thousands,
If I knew
That at nightfall
All my soil would shrink
To an island
And all my crowds
To you.

CAROL LYNN PEARSON

Your Voice

I would take your voice
And fill a tub with it
And soak in it for hours.

The vowels and consonants
And little laughs
Would articulate around me,
A sound sauna,
Caressing and deep.

And then I would
Take your voice
And roll it out
Like a blanket
And lie down in it
And let it hum me
To sleep.

Embrace

I think
I have melted
All over you—
Melted like a crayon
On a windowsill
On a warm, warm day.

You may have to
Peel me off.
Or let me stay.

Like the Weather

Drenched and dripping
I tell you
That love is rather
Like the weather—

Something you can
Report on,
But not very well
Control.

Don't Touch

It's all right, really,
That I touch you?

Somehow I look around
For signs you might see
In a museum
Or wherever else they
House the world's
Extraordinary things.

I could only look
At the Rembrandts
And the Chinese vases,
And I could not
Get closer than three feet
To the crown jewels.

Well, I didn't even want to.
But you?
It would be asking too much
For me to be in a room with you
And not touch.

 CAROL LYNN PEARSON

It's all right?
I can sit on this couch
With your head in my lap
And trace your eyebrows
And lips and face?
I can play with your hair like this?
And even kiss
And tickle if I want
And no one will call a guard?

Why do I smile
Like I'm getting away
With something bold?

There were alarms fixed in case
I should try to touch
King Tut's face—
And his was only gold.

Blown

You have blown like feathers
Across the landscape
Of my life.

I could not gather you now
If I wanted—

You are
Too many
And too far.

Winner

By what fortune
Did I win you?

Here in the morning paper
Is a woman waving
The winning ticket in
A million-dollar lottery.

Was I lucky too?

Or is it possible that through
Some forgotten merit
I earned you
Like the man across the page
Earned his Nobel Prize?

Well, I won.
And with more than
Million-dollar marvel
In my eyes
I shall take my winnings
And run.

The Sigh

I have figured out
The sigh,
The lover's sigh.

It is a mortal's futile attempt
In an ecstatic moment
To live forever
Like the gods do,
Breathing only in
As if to lift to heaven—

And then dumbly, numbly
Dropping back to earth
In a smiling expiration.

Filled

My life was a jar,
Packed with pebbles
To the top.

I didn't know
There were spaces
Until you filled them.

Like sand filtering
The empty places
Full,
You are there between
And around every thought,
Every motion.

There is no moment
That is not
Heavy with you somehow.
I am pressed,
Pressed.

Even breathing
Is not easy now.

Cliché

I hated clichés
Until I fell in love.
But now I see they're true,
All true.

For I want to love you,
My love,
At the earliest possible opportunity,
Up one side and down the other.

I want to love you
Until I'm blue in the face.

I want to love you
In no uncertain terms,
Bag and baggage,
Whole hog,
Warp and woof,
Kit and caboodle,
Tooth and nail,
Hammer and tongs,
Root and branch,
Lock, stock and barrel,

From pillar to post,
Let the chips fall where they may.

And let me say, my love,
That when all has been
Said and done—

I want to love you
In every way, shape and form,
First, last and always,
Until the cows come home.

Gratitude

Do I say
Thank you for loving me
Like I say
Thank you for the butter?

(I didn't say please
In the first place.)

If I say
Thank you for loving me
Do you then say
You're welcome?
We would both laugh at that.

Thank you
Doesn't do it at all.
Words are strange things.

But things that are not strange
And that are not words
Are written in my eyes.
When you come
Close enough to read them
You will know.

I will hold my gratitude
Until then.

The Choir

There is a choir in me
That unpredictably
Breaks into hymns
Of praise for your being.

Graciously
I keep the sound on low
So everyone else can go
About their business
And not know
What they're missing.

With You

I want to be with you
More than I want
To wake up in the morning,
And I like waking up.

But having stirred into
Life behind life,
Having lifted my hand
In the shine
Of a new sun,
Having been filled
And thrilled with something
Finer than oxygen—

I could not go back
To merely breathing
Again.

Seeing You Seeing Me

Seeing you seeing me
Took my breath away.

I never knew
There were Grand Canyons
In me,
And Mona Lisas
And Sistine Chapels
And the Alps—

Until that look,
That amazed, amazing look,
Crossed your tourist face
And I became the newest
Wonder of the world.

Tangible

Being in love
Is a tangible thing.
It wakes me from sleep
Like fingers on my face,
Or like the turning over
Of a lover
For a middle of the night
Embrace.

Touching You

I do not touch you
To make you happy.
Let me admit that right off.

I touch the people
At the rest home
To make them happy.
I rub their shoulders
And stroke their hair
And they smile.

But touching you?
That is about as charitable
As eating my own supper
Or breathing my own air
Or placing my body
Between clean sheets.

And if some day
In some rest home
You find me
Rubbing your shoulders
And stroking your hair,
Anyone watching will see
It's only a little for you.
Mostly for me.

When You Kiss Me

When you kiss me
I cannot believe
In death.

When you kiss me
I believe that love and life
Are always
And that all the funerals
I have seen
Were only bad dreams.

We will not die,
Will we?

There will not be a time,
Will there be,
When I won't feel
The wonderful warmth
Of your breath?

All I know
Is that when you kiss me
I cannot believe
In death.

Silently

Please understand
That if I sit
And look at you
Silently

I am processing
Your presence

And conversation would
Feel as strange to me
As talking with
My mouth full.

Just silently
Let me be.

Beads

I string the moments
We have spent together
Like beads
And reverence them
As one might
Reverence a rosary.

Fingers caress and polish
With grateful care—
Each a blessing,
Each a prayer.

Sunbather

The knowledge
Of your love
Hangs high and bright.

I,
A sunbather,
Too white
From too long a winter,
Shiver into warmth
And strain
Toward the sky.

Kiss

Kiss is not
An onomatopoeic word.
It does not sound like itself
At all.

Buzz does.
Whirr does.
Sizzle does.
But *kiss* is too close
To *hiss*, which also does.

The word I want
Should not have sibilants,
And nothing so hard
As a *k*.
Soft, soft sounds.

M's would be nice
Or *N*'s.
And a vowel that almost
Faints with pleasure,
Oh, *ou* or *ah*.

Perhaps the great *Ohmm*
From India would work.
Ohmm. I like that.

It might sound strange
On the radio:
"Gimme a little ohmm,
Will ya, huh?"

Well,
I don't need the word at all
When I'm with you.
Don't talk.
Just do.

The Signal

In case of crowds
Or other muffling
Circumstances,
I've designed a sign
That should get through:

If you notice me
Breathing,
That will signal
I love you.

Not Gardeners

I would weed you
Of your pain.
I would reach in
With bare hands
And take it by the roots,
Leaving you clear and clean
And thriving.

But even lovers
Are not gardeners
To any plots but their own.
Pain is such a private thing.

I will stand close
And throw
Flowers across the fence
On the chance
That some will go to seed
And grow.

Sabbatical

One ought not
To have to work
When one is in love—

Except perhaps
At something quite automatic
Like doing the dishes
Or cleaning out the car.

But nothing
That requires the mind.
I find, these days,
That I can push a project
Only so far before
I collide with you.
Project flies off
In one direction,
You and I fly off
In another.

I back up,
Try again,
And then—.

One ought not
To have to work
When one is in love.

It's a disability
And there's no use trying.
Society should offer
A sabbatical to lovers
For the purpose of
Staring out of windows
And sighing.

Energy Source

This energy
That warms and lights
Originates,
I suppose,
Out there somewhere
Like the bright stuff
That springs from the sky
To the kitchen.

And so if it comes
Not from you
But through you,
That's all right with me.

You do conduct it
Beautifully.

Thoughts

Thoughts are things
And words have wings.
I love you
And I think it
In the thousands—

Wondering
What you must feel,
Kissed by swarms of
Gentle, unseen stings,
Brushed and rushed
By strangely real
Flocks of warm
And winged things.

No Business

I have no business
Being in your life.

But I am not here
On business—
I am here on love.
And love transacts
Without permission.

Love does not phone ahead
Or even knock.
It just shows up
And sits down
And takes over
And lets some in
And turns some away.

It let me in
And wrote me in red
All over your calendar.

And so,
Although I have no business
Being in your life,
I may stay
Anyway.

Love Letters

It's a shame—
All this tenderness
Callously tossed into
Your mailbox
Between a utilities bill
And an ad
For motor tune-ups.

The postal service,
I propose,
Should have a special line
For love letters,
Should send them
The scenic route,
And deliver them
At sunset
With dignity
And—where possible—
A rose.

CAROL LYNN PEARSON

Warm

I love
Being in love with you.

It's warm,
Like a sweater
I have knitted for you
And wear until
I can give it to you.

It's a little big for me.
But warm.

Hungry

I am hungry for you.

I press against
Time and space
Like an unfed
Child against
A window that is
Clear and thick
Between her eyes
And bread.

No Matter

Is the lesson, then,
Mind over matter?

Your matter
Is far too far away
To give me warmth.
(Puppies do not huddle well
Hundreds of miles apart.)

Still—
This incredible comfort,
Warmer even than skin,
Covers me like a quilt.

In that other way of being,
Mind, spirit, heart—
We huddle very well,
Hundreds of miles apart.

Your Name

I love to write
Your name on envelopes.

It's like I'm creating you
Letter by letter,
And in a moment
There you are
Complete in cursive
Before my very eyes.

I write you out
Reverently,
Each line, each twist
A private little proof
That you exist.

All My Love

When I sign
My letters to you
"All my love,"
I don't mean it,
You know.

I save some
For sunsets and philosophy
And warm baths
And the theatre
And brown paper packages
Tied up with strings
And friends and giraffes,
In fact all creatures
Great and small
And other things.

So where I write
"All my love,"
Read "All the rest of,"
Which is maybe eighty percent of,
Which is a lot.

Unembodied

My love for you
Is weary of the spirit world.

It has gone unembodied
For so long,
A little ghost
That has learned
All it can
As wind that moves
But does not touch.

It hovers now
As close as it's allowed
To earth,
And holds its breath
For birth.

Magic

You materialized
Out of the mist
Better than Houdini
Could have done it—
Molecule after molecule
Exploding into place
In a fine rush of matter
That left you solidly
In space.

Magic, I hear,
Is done with mirrors.
But you are too warm
To be glass.

And I am too
Mesmerized
To ask.

Meditation

You are my mantra.
You repeat over and over
In my mind
Like a lovely sound,
Leading me further
And further within.

You rest there
At the center,
More fixed and flickering
Than the candle,
More many-petaled
Than the lotus.

I study you.
I vibrate with you.
I am restored in you.

Occupied

Loving you
Gives me something to do
When I'm waiting in line
And forgot to bring a book
And don't even have
My nail clippers.

If asked
They would say
I'm sitting here
Doing nothing.

Not true.
Occupied:
Loving you.

Not Guilty

Should you and I feel guilty
To be so full
When so many are empty?

I would share, and I do.
But redistribution of love
Is harder even than
Redistribution of wealth.

Look at it this way:
If you and I are filled,
There are two less people
On the welfare rolls.
The system has cause
To be thrilled.

Waking

The opening curtain
Shudders, moves
On an unseen cue.

The stage
Is consciousness,
The cast is you.

Home

Outside your arms
Is a place
I like to visit
But I wouldn't want
To live there.

This is home now,
This small cozy structure
We build of an embrace.
This is comfort—
It is fireplace, lamp,
And softest chair.

I will go out
From time to time
For exercise and such
And to keep in touch
With the world where people
Eat and laugh and work.

CAROL LYNN PEARSON

But I'm a stranger there now,
A stranger in a strange land,
And I never get warm enough
And I'm always alone.

Then—
The touch of your hand,
And I know I'm nearly home.

Eyes

I was never one
For looking into eyes,
Not straight into them
For any length of time.

Was I afraid
That if I left the door
Too wide too long
Something would be stolen,
Or maybe something left
That I wouldn't like?

And why can I
Now look into your eyes
For what feels forever?

I guess at last
I trust the traffic—
And so enjoy the pleasure
Of the air.

Without You

Even air is thick
With you now.

A world without you
Would be
Like Mercury or Mars,
An atmosphere
Too thin for life
Somehow.

My Context

You love me
Out of context.
You love me as a noun
Lifted from sentence,
Paragraph, page.

But seeing me
Surrounded by
All my other nouns,
My verbs, adverbs, adjectives,
And now and again
An expletive—
Would you love me then?

Or could you love me
Maybe, even more?

CAROL LYNN PEARSON

When you have found
How complex compound
My structure is,
When you have seen
My meaning multiply
And multiply,
When you know
Not only where
I am written
But how I function—
Would you,
Could you care to join me
In some marvelous
Conjunction?

Could I Sleep

Could I sleep
If I slept with you?
Could I forget
The fact of your skin
Within touching distance
Long enough to let go?

Lovers do sleep,
I know.
I've seen it in the movies.

But just now,
Riveted awake merely
By the thought of you,
I can't imagine how.

The Rest

After I have felt with you
All that it's possible
To feel—

After I have said to you
All that it's possible
To say—

What then—
An aria?
A ballet?

Or may I just breathe my way
Into stillness
And let you
Guess the rest?

Double Wedding

Let's have a double wedding,
You and me
And eros and agape.

Let us post
Interchangeable notes
On bedroom wall
And refrigerator:
"Love thy lover"
And "Love thy neighbor."

Let us hold hands
In movies
And in the hospital.

Let us kiss
Shoulders and eyelids
And the cut fingers
Of small children.

Let us serve one another
Apple blossoms in vases
And quartered fruit
On trays.

Let us write poems
And wills to each other.
Let us have nights
As friendly lovers
And days as loving friends.

And let the four of us,
You and me
And eros and agape,
Stand in line together,
At the grocery store
And at a golden
Anniversary.

Work Around It

Is it hard
To kiss me
When I'm smiling?

An attempt to control
Might only compound it.

You may just have to
Work around it.

Leavened

You settled in my life
Like a yeast
And rose and rose
And keep on rising.

Nothing has been
So strangely alive before.
Daily I am leavened
More.

Handicapped

I hesitate to talk about
Being in love
To someone who is not.

It suddenly feels
Rude somehow,
Like dancing around
A wheelchair
Or parading a rainbow
Before a blind person.

I have an impulse
To say something
Comforting and ridiculous
Like one might say
To the handicapped—
Or just to drop my eyes
And turn away.

Love as Pantomime

Love as pantomime
Lacks something.

Oh, I could act it out
For hours, dumbly,
Happily,
And you would know all,
All without words.

But they come, these words,
They press their way toward sound,
And between kisses
I let them through—
Not for information,
But for celebration:

"I love you.
Oh, I love you,
Love you."

Different

There are
Millions of women,
I know,
Who get along without you.

They manage
To go through a complete day
Without thinking of you
Even once,
Filling their lives
Somehow
With things and thoughts
That are not you,
Out there in their
Millions of homes and offices
And shops and rice paddies.

Millions of women
Who in one way or another
Can mold some meaning
Into life without you.

Now,
I do not mean
To make fun of them.

It's just that—
I am not one of them.

One Skin

It is lovely to be
Nearly one skin,
Not knowing
Quite where you leave off
And I begin—

Like a watercolor
That runs the blues
Of sea and sky.

Some mystic brush
Has been at work,
Erasing lines,
Embracing spaces,
Bordering us only by bliss.

I want never again
To know where you leave off
And I begin.

To Know You

I would read you
Like braille,
Pore over you
By day and by night
Until all your themes
And subtle meanings
Were understood.

To know you
Would be good.

Let Me Bless You

I am better than
All things medical,
You know.

My touch is charged
With love
Which is light
Which is life.

My touch goes inches in,
Way past skin
To gland and bone
And marrow even.

I am not practicing
Without a license
Or competing with
The men in white.

Take their tests
And tablets
And treatments.
Drop sugar.
Eat raw or slightly steamed.

Study herbs and yoga
And every healing art.

Then come—
And let me bless you
With the laying on
Of hands
And lips
And heart.

To the Sound of the Rain

I want to love you tonight
To the sound of the rain.

I want to be
Roof and walls to you,
And burning wood.

I want you to see my smile
For a second of lightning.

I want you to hear
The steady beat of my heart
Between the thunder
And my voice
Whispering your name
And almost silent kisses
As I love you tonight
To the sound of the rain.

I Would Rather Kiss You

Why would I rather
Kiss you
Than count money, even?

I have lost all ambition,
All drive to do
Wonderful things.

It is truly disgusting
And decadent
And I admit it—

A bright and talented
Human being
With energy only
To reach once more
For your mouth.

Assimilated

I have
Assimilated you
Somehow.

You are no longer
Something there
That I observe,
But something here
Like my hands
Or my hair—

A part of me
I hardly notice,
But could hardly spare.

Essence of Love

I splash your love on me
Like perfume—
Lavish
The lovelier than lilac scent
Over wrists and temples
And neck.

Heads turn
As I walk.

Activist

Perhaps after all
There is no better way
To improve the world
Than this, just lying here
In your arms.

Nuns shower grace
As real as rain upon the earth
With their prayers.

Meditators overflow
Their chakras with a river
Of calm that rolls on
Its cleansing way.

And lovers?
Perhaps these moments
Of ecstasy
Rise like birds
From their nests
To outsing the storm.

Lie down, my love.
There are earthquakes
In Spain.
There is war
In the Middle East.

The call is out
For all nuns, meditators
And lovers
To close their eyes
And bring peace.

Filling You

I want to fill my days
With filling you.

I am acres of wheat.
Let me harvest, mill
Mix, rise, bake, spread
With honey
And serve you
Breakfast in bed.

Focus

Falling in love
Is a matter of focus
I believe—
Like a movie camera that
Zooms in on a face
Leaving everyone else
Background and slightly
Blurred.

The story calls for it:
One face
Suddenly the only face.

Ingenious and
Absurd.

Sabbath

And you are
My Sabbath too.

I come to you for rest
Renewal—
Come to worship God in you
And God in me.

Silently
As light through the religious reds
And blues and golds of glass
In a cathedral window

I come to you for peace.

The Rhyme

We are cosmically correct
And I love you.

We have karma to collect
And I love you.

Sometime
I'll know the reason.
Just now I feel
The rhyme.

And I love you.

What You Do to Me

Recent medical literature
indicates people are healthier
when they're in love.

My darling
At the thought of you
The lactic acid in my blood drops
Making me less tired.

At your touch, my love
My endorphins increase
Producing a natural sense of
Well-being.

As your arms go around me
The lymphocytes go wild
In my blood
Strengthening my white cells.

And, oh
With your lips on mine
My limbic system is charged
And activity is increased
In all parts of my body.

And so, my love
I am grateful for you
From the bottom of my liver
And lungs and pancreas
And every other part—

Not to mention, my love
My heart.

Loving You

I could do without
Your loving me
Better than I could
Do without my loving you.

Your love
Warms me from
The outside in.
But mine warms me from
The inside out
And out and out.

I cannot give up giving
Now that I have learned
How glorious it feels
To fall on someone
Like sunlight.

I could not do
Without loving you.

CAROL LYNN PEARSON

Final Comfort

Knowing that I will die sometime,
I want to tell you that you will be
My final comfort.

They may put small pieces
Of ice in my mouth,
But I will be with you and candles
And music slow enough to kiss to.

They may apply oxygen,
But I will be with you,
Laughing and breathing hard
As we reach the top of the hill.

They may feel my feet
And put another cover on,
But, oh, my love, I shall be warm.

They will press my eyelids closed
With careful fingertips
And lift the sheet over the smile
On my lips.